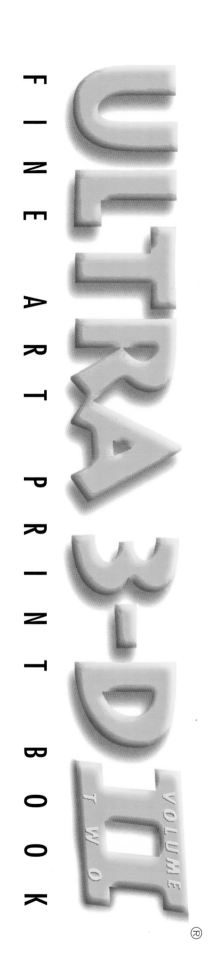

ULTRA 3-D II

FINE ART PRINT BOOK

VOLUME TWO ®

ULTRA 3-D ®

Front Line Art Publishing
Montage Publications Division • Quarto Publishing
San Diego, California • London, England

ISBN: 1-56714-030-0

First Printing, November 1994

3-D Artists:

We are currently preparing a new 3-D book.

Please send submissions to:

MONTAGE PUBLICATIONS
3-D ART SUBMISSIONS
9808 WAPLES STREET
SAN DIEGO, CALIFORNIA 92121 USA

Include self-addressed stamped envelope.

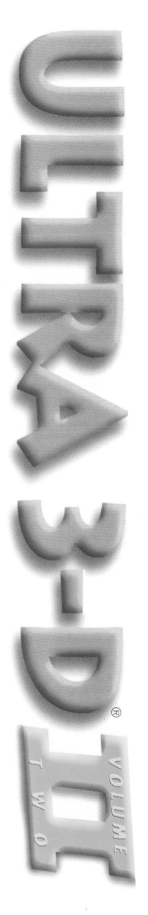

FOREWARD

Welcome to the second volume of ULTRA 3-D®, a new and challenging art form. Although 3-D images and stereograms have been around for decades in many different forms, we have now entered the age where we need only our eyes and minds to create amazing illusions of depth. This new art form is so visually stimulating, you will find yourself actually reaching out to touch the images that seem so real just beyond the printed page.

From the very first page of ULTRA 3-D II®, you realize that you are in for a fantastic ride. Through a wonderous mix of art and science, these amazing images will transport you to 25 different worlds, each with incredible detail and depth. As you stare at the fields of colors, lines and patterns, they will begin to swirl, move and separate when suddenly...

You are bounding with the hunters of the wild

through rocky canyons.

You are gazing out across the African Plains

with the unchallenged rulers of their domain.

You are gliding along with mystical mermaids

and playful dolphins in their underwater playground.

You are standing on the deck of a 16th century

schooner, watching in amazement as majestic whales

crash through the rolling waves.

Ultra 3-D II® has been created for everyone. An innovative and creative challenge to the most sophisticated viewer, and a relaxing experience for those who wish to enjoy a unique, new art form.

Enjoy

ULTRA 3-D II® art by Marty Engle, Johnny Ray Barnes Jr., Francois Guerin
Cover design by Marty Engle, Johnny Ray Barnes Jr.

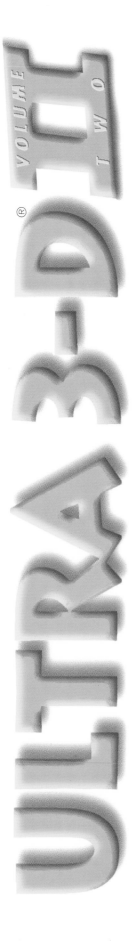

ULTRA 3-D II

VOLUME TWO

When viewed properly, Stereograms and 3-D art prints can spring to mind many pleasant surprises. Remember to relax (both the mind and eye) and have patience. There are several ways to view the prints depending on size and format:

GENERAL VIEWING INSTRUCTIONS:

View at eye level. Stand at a medium distance from the image (2 to 4 ft.). Concentrate on your reflection or the reflection of light on the image. Stare THROUGH the picture as if you were looking at something a distance BEHIND the image. Keep focused on one area of the image. Depending on eyesight of the viewer, different lengths of time may be required for the image to become clear. CONTINUE STARING as the image will appear. When the pattern begins to move or shift the image is about to form. If you have trouble seeing the image, try standing with your nose just touching the print. Stare at the print at this distance and keep your eyes fixed at that position while slowly backing away from the print. Continue backing away until the image begins to form. Be patient as it takes some practice.

IF THE PRINT IS BEHIND GLASS:

· Start by looking at your own reflection in the glass cover.
· Then look beyond the reflection into the back of the picture, as if you are looking through a window.
· Keep staring through the picture. Once you see the image the first time, it becomes easier to see it again.

IF THE PRINT HAS NO REFLECTIVE SURFACE:

· Hold the print just at the end of your nose. Let your eyes relax and let the picture be out of focus. Just keep staring through the picture, not at it.
· Slowly move the print away from your face, continuing to look through the picture. Stop at a comfortable reading distance.
· When you start to see an image come into focus, keep staring through it.

AN ALTERNATIVE TECHNIQUE:

· Focus on an object in the distance.
· Maintaining that focal point, insert the print between your eyes and the distant object.
· The print will be blurry, but that's OK. Keep your eyes focused exactly as they are, staring blankly, without actually "looking" at anything.
· Move the print slowly forward and backward.
· When the print reaches the right position, the three-dimensional image will come into focus.

CALL OF THE WILD

PERFECT DAY FOR SAILING

ON THE HUNT

DAISIES

ENCHANTED FORTRESS

5

FIGHTER PLANES

FLIGHT OF THE HUNTER

SOMEWHERE IN THE HEART

8

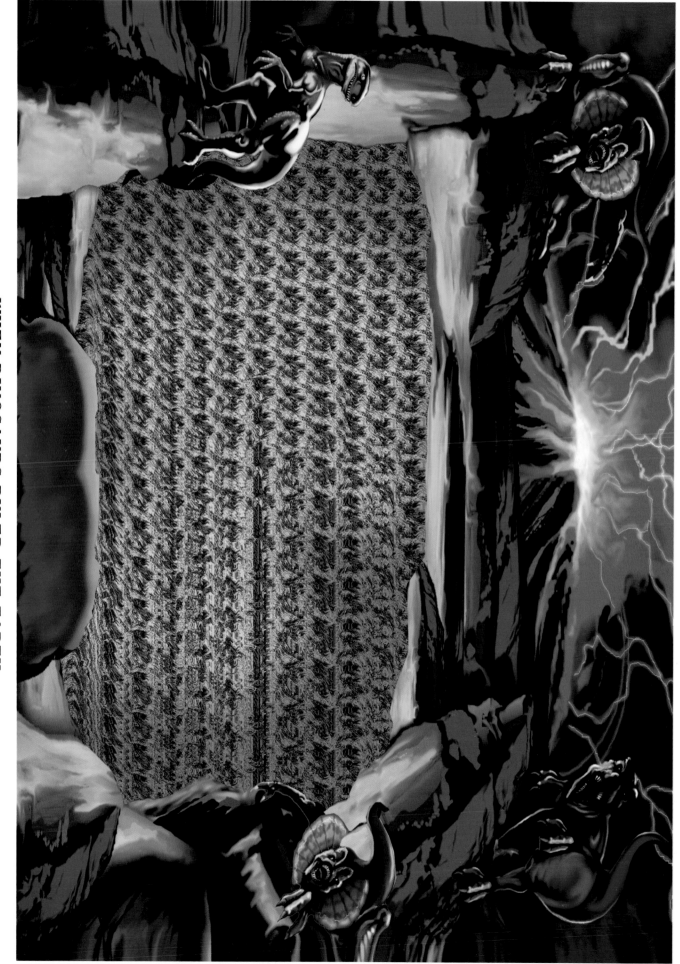

WHEN DINOSAURS RULED THE EARTH

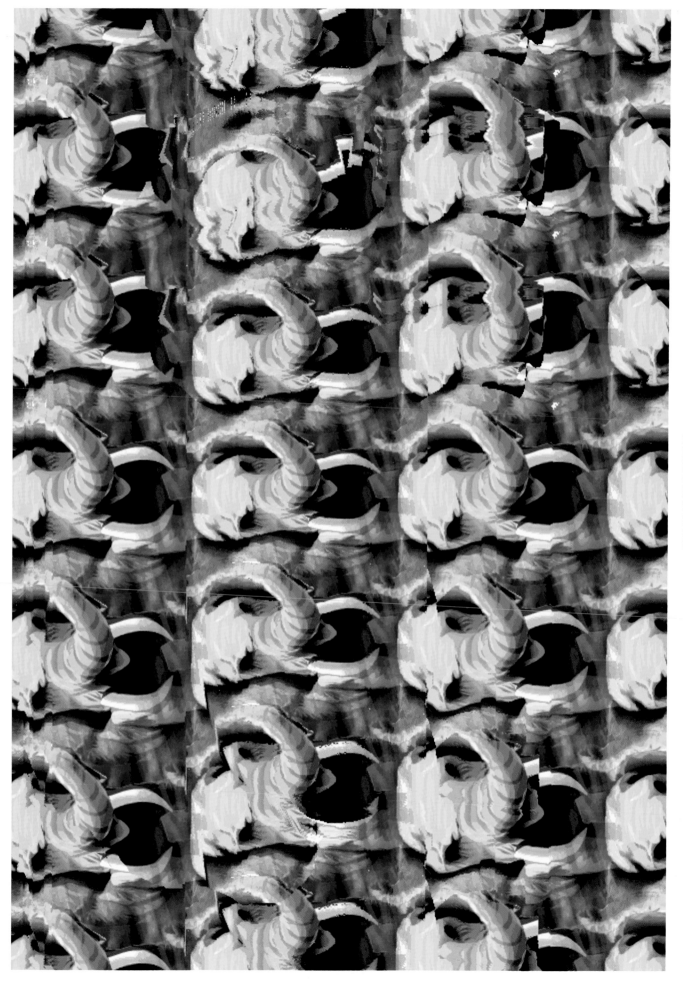

ELEPHANTS

NOBLE KING

LOVESTRUCK

MONSTER TRUCK

WHEN I THINK OF YOU

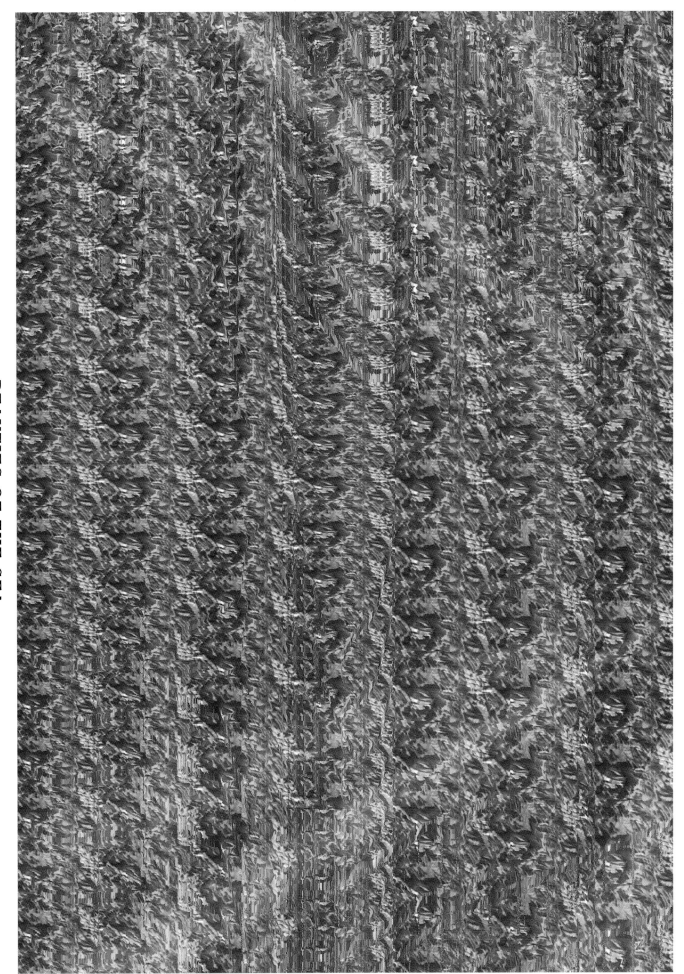

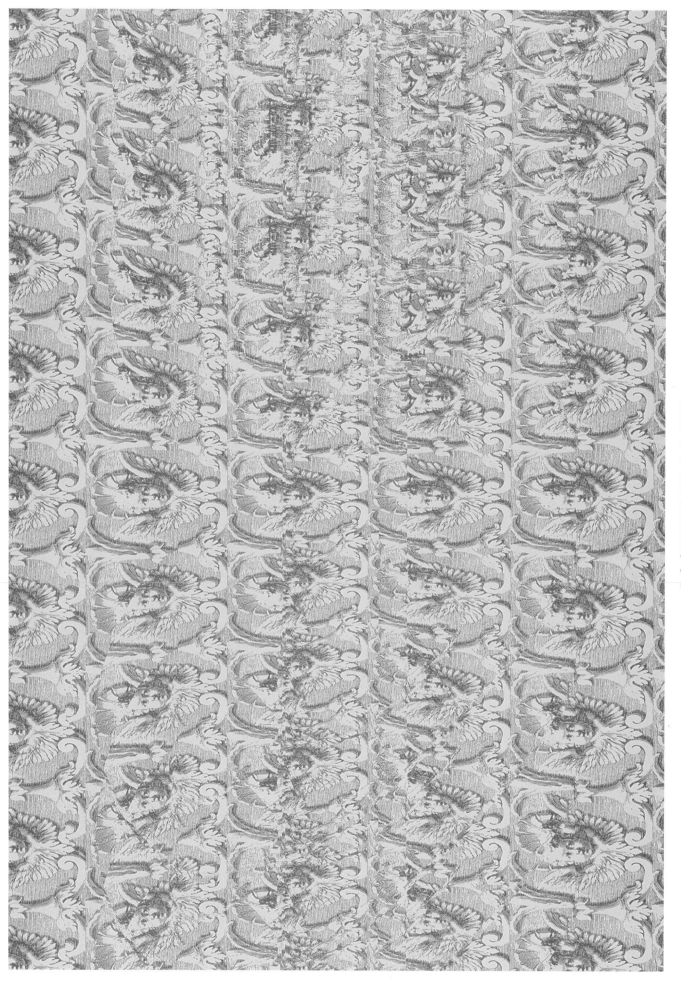

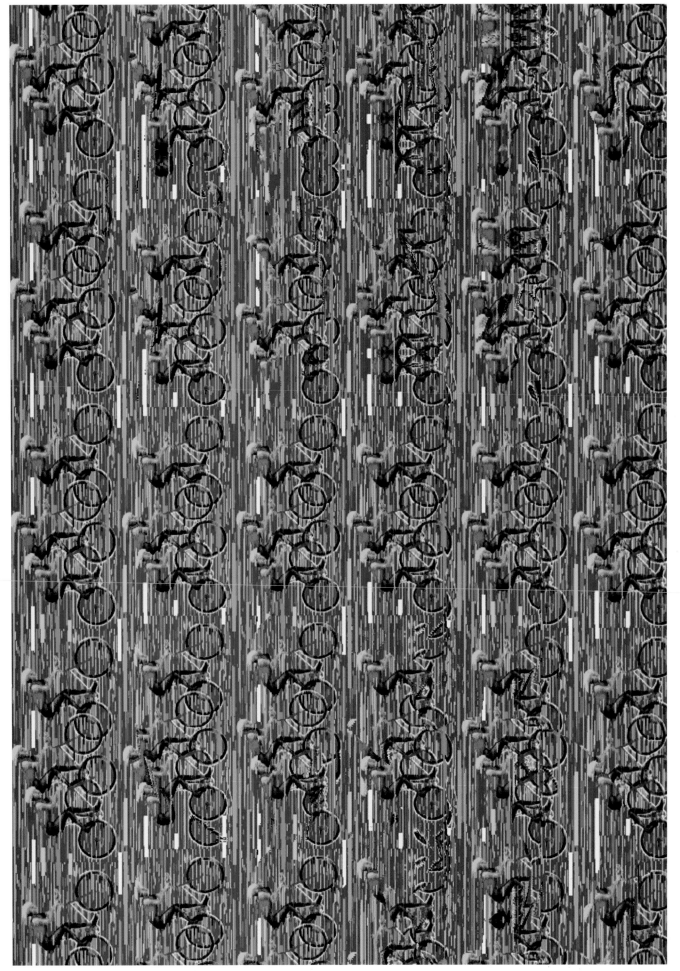

BICYCLES

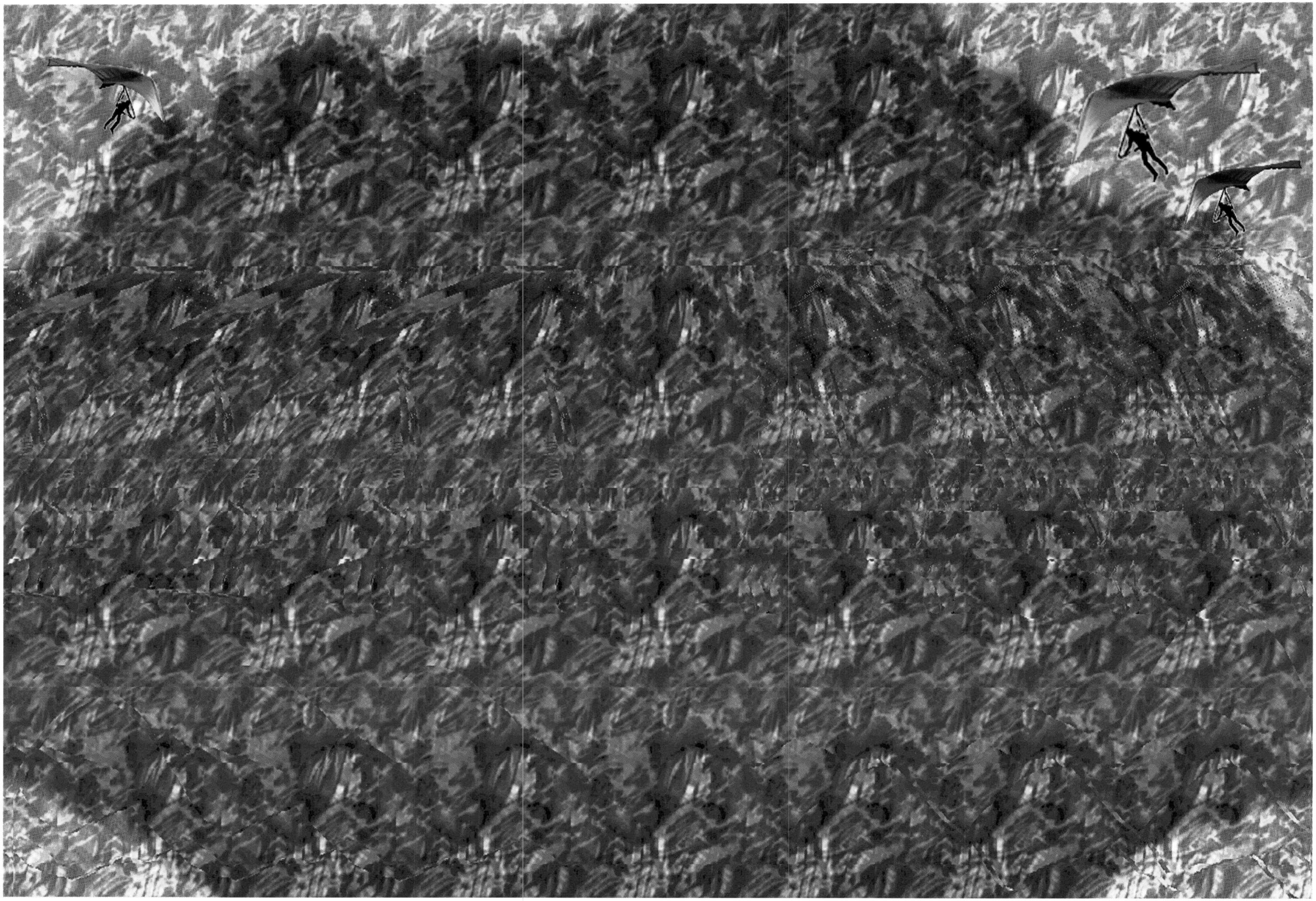

LOOK TO THE SKIES

PANDA

RED ROSES

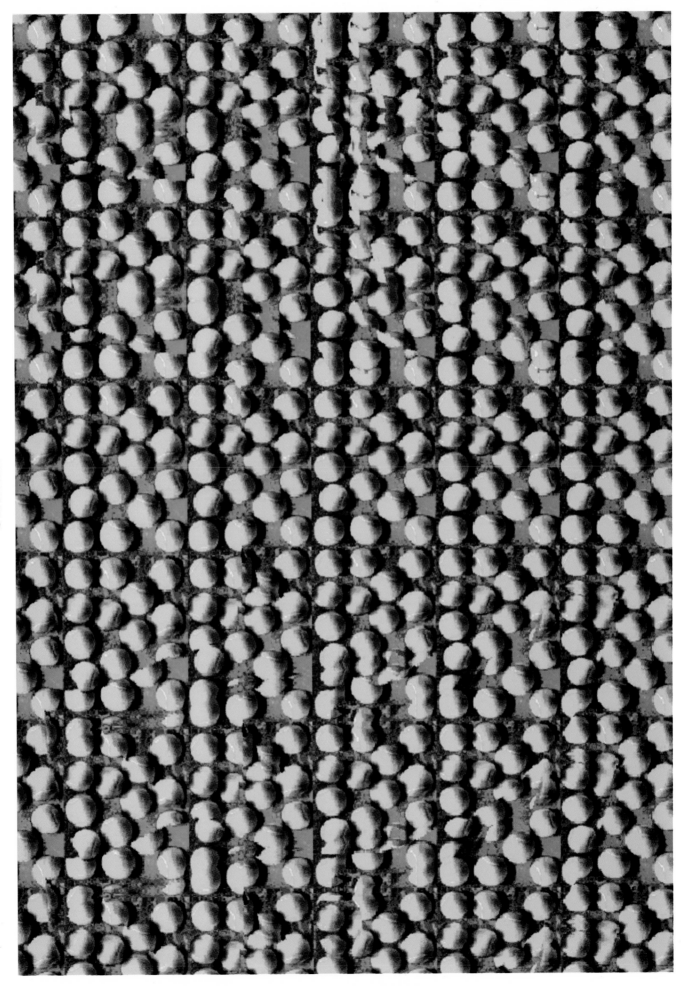

TENNIS

AIRBORNE

ULTRA 3-D II

HIDDEN IMAGES

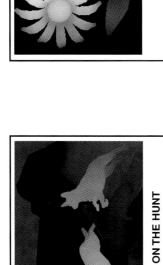

DAISIES

4

ON THE HUNT

3

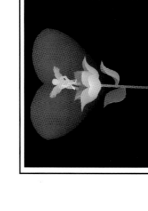
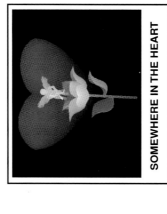

PERFECT DAY FOR SAILING

2

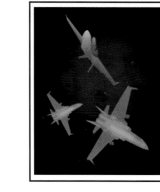

CALL OF THE WILD

1

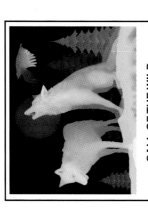

SOMEWHERE IN THE HEART

8

FLIGHT OF THE HUNTER

7

FIGHTER PLANES

6

ENCHANTED FORTRESS

5

LOVESTRUCK

12

NOBLE KING

11

ELEPHANTS

10

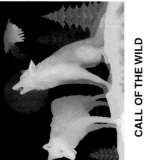

WHEN DINOSAURS RULED
THE EARTH

9

ULTRA 3-D II

VOLUME TWO

HIDDEN IMAGES

13 MONSTER TRUCK

17 FANTASTIC ENCOUNTER

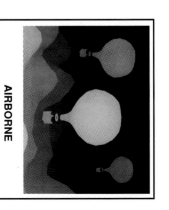

21 PANDA

14 WHEN I THINK OF YOU

18 BICYCLES

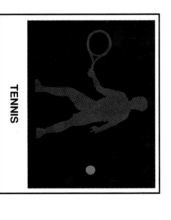

22 RED ROSES

15 BEAUTIES OF THE SEA

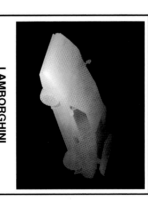

19 LAMBORGHINI

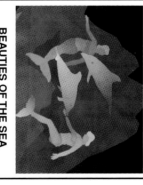

23 TENNIS

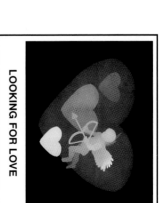

16 LOOKING FOR LOVE

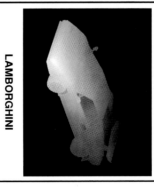

20 LOOK TO THE SKIES

24 AIRBORNE

SEE YOU NEXT TIME